AF880435

Corpus Socius

ahsahta press

The New Series

number 1

Corpus Socius

poems by

Lance Phillips

ahsahta press

Boise State University • Boise, Idaho • 2002

Ahsahta Press, Boise State University
Boise, Idaho 83725
http://ahsahtapress.boisestate.edu

Copyright © 2002 by Lance Phillips

Printed in the United States of America
Cover art by Martin Corless-Smith, "Odilon Redone: Study after *Armure*"
First printing 2002
ISBN 0-916272-71-0

Library of Congress Cataloging-in-Publication Data

Phillips, Lance, 1970 –
Corpus socius: poems / by Lance Phillips.
p. cm.
ISBN 0-916272-71-0 (pbk. : alk. paper)
I. Title.
PS3616.H46 C67 2002
811'.6--dc21

2001007695

For Kelly and Caden

Contents

Acknowledgments

Some of these texts first appeared in *Colorado Review, Fence,* and *Interim*.

Already

A more common sparrow being heat on the wing

The tongue's little more a sun   I don't know how

Subsequent heron numbers the which and bridge among
shall

Snow's future flees

I was honest among simple   between breast, sheet

Below run-off a slick a transient of

The cell's moral am: yes
Different from private is and the bee is cross-sectioned

∞

Yes moral am, yes from   Day-box strikes you
catalpa, lymph   My mouths my

The how

Secularist, am says head
says diagram from I
bulks poppy

Sunday's new sheet   or
that her lip rose up—seizes   iris
                                        riseup
that her lip rose up—seized
frees the genital disproportionate sparrow
                                                    (in argument)
trust and belly in O   (boys seize him)

That nailrise daily up

Brother's arch one rib

Here's snowing so gulch of grass
crocus plus face

∞

False spring, endocrine lord's I frontal matter—is lentil

∞

Am's pair cilia, perch was behaviorist

Retinalbud flurry its acetylene petal flanks
Why saint simon stock it's what grace is

Signifies two wings the plural

Such that a sunfigure
At liberties wheatberry yeast
Does
Doe hears a possum
Do I over a bee's posture

∞

Two hawks m′ experimentally

Mount carmel.   Hushwell
tabling some tulips
belong

Isle/I'll. Softest disc the sun

If need be pigeon, erudition belong

∞

Anselm burning's the grass infallible

∞

Felt today Jesus distinctly beneath right shoulder
blade in the muscle along my spine while rotating
right hand clockwise 1] crowds her
2] branch
3] es (straw)
4] the genital

Seem

That salt was and necessary
Grammarian the car —fishes
Am fishes pups a local one
I'm versus two   as my son
Cord's bulbing moon, queen
anne's lace words/weaves
conditioned response yes: yes

Crooked nail, nonconformist
in which moon, slitting rims
I have used similitudes: is,
two moths as you my elation
In which moon, slitting seems

∞

As trusts, as tree
now go the sun under wood
Dogwood's Blake's lifemask
as trusts, as treed is lyric

∞

Three geese hybrid she's/I'm. 1] wing 2] segmented body 3] wing

Jesus however's holy—
mastersingings: 1] soil
2] cuticle plus trowel
3] madrigals one only
be there dogwood 4]
so scapula, the iris's before
deduced 5] thus mica's, air's
contusion frees I'm hearing

—

6] bullet 7] A bullet lifts-lifting
8] her 9] dahlia words this
spine's a stem

Faminizing sun
aleph kidney
weir wants crossing
thus shell   apprehending
weed splendors weed

                    guttural sun
came   I come honestly
rema(r)king   say sun

Irides Jesus the joy

Accretes I where pavilion
bicyclist is landscape
Greenfly filling fills virtue
/opensky/
Irides Jesus rejoice

Jawing
three rains
syllabic
only manages I
fern
along the creek

along builds
a snap dragon
bench tin bells
manages one
who arches always

Green halter what its jawing roots
1] and seeing only
2] birch and moved

The human being

Safed goldenrod:
safed field's
a telling   Whose
fifth remove: road
babe and hoof

Moth is such I'm brutalizing

So simulating as alyssum
and turnip are crucifiers   I've come

—the goldfinch hoisting error
and away   Remembrancing I've not vs. the lea

Where the lake the clock
fettering buttock, along
the spine and courage
      vs. a vanity of
the fail promising

Anvil's promiser   Alike the gain this morning beginning
tickseed, aurora
The happier for the muscle

Portion's sweetest root

A space between sweet pea 2 pinecones
The cord-rot snapped, preempting one step and frost
The hounds along the fence give honest meaning: a cyst
and a spade

The acts   I've immediate acts
Cloud full with hand then mouth's
a lightning of mercury of hair's memorable lust

3.

11 burnings of bushes outwardize the regular sun
squirrel the tongue again

Ninth countenance: a trade over

lessening against the birch
Her fingerline safes horizon,
the weir rushing to surface ice, twigs
Half an inch of ice is the patience

Kept the grasses with the smiter's dialogue
with half a tree left insulating the ground

∞

The acknowledging pigeon's no gaze

Could carry no one in between

Snow's threat both
reduced crooked arm
the bell
with eye movement
third in five days
as by a bird, there
centered the butterfly on death
out from his hand his attention

And at removes
some writing with the cold, breathable air
begging into fuel resurrects out the pine knot

5.

So able with section
with sheaf, forehead
with causation

Orbis sensualim pictus

Valued sun outside from isolation

∞

 Where trunk
diaphragm agree delineating
across the spine not even
bruised I, the origin's supplement

Axon sustaining plum-reflex its branch has embodied

8.

A
with judgment in the immediacy of A
lapses to goldeye, to possum

∞

so
values the stripped branch
has valued the outstripped branch
better   The squirrel
I know shape of his hand
nearer, variable

The only word for a body

1] Anti-electron, titmouse turn by acceleration
2] the agent
3] cogitansmouth extensamouth

The titmouse, anti-electron
accelerate maple
cogitansmouth thinning to a nest

Pigeonthroat
re-potentiates the living
for moisture,
self-judgment

2] Cat's rib part carcass
the sun fell from
attention 3] I am afraid

When   when
congestive with lilacs
                    inaction

∞

    Distinguishes men, raccoon
the one hind quarter rigorous in making attention
new space
Four emptyings as such

A plant near the churchyard

On the one the swollen index
veery's dustbath outlines *y*

———

  How
sure with a
with flagpole, coagula
with content

A third time in my peripheral vision Jesus's
fine-indigo-grid rushing toward then away

Stillest form the engram's blue flag

∞

Not suffering but the distinction of all things
      bring along the nets
physicality lord garment

A's

valley
recollapses the small girls
up, back to the puddles

Intaking
at cheek microstructure

dee de de
At abundance

Identity

    Each tulip
or -ides authority
putty, latch, pane glass
each *e* put loudly

∞

Oughtsides the one rose
Iphigenia
Gain's thumbs' muscles

Judgment's now veery, now spout
legitimizing such hop
Counterpoise

With *i* in my name
Stephanas's family/
household synthesizes
sun, proline
else nest's hole

Just start sometime
Gaius with the word parataxis

Physically rims the pre-exfoliated rose
with three ants, dust, Ephesus
suring, self-imaging the ants

Little claw demiraclizing earth
through digging into him
yea yea socius
rims desiring lavender familiar
rose with whiteflies
with the answer toward death

∞

With *i* from out socius
mole, their bright hinges
down before it pressing into it
being anarchical at the pressure into
putting forward crush, rigor

Red glads, table
with that pressure
ready receiving ts
from out insurrectionists

∞

New sparrow patterns ants to the moment

Difference

Milkeye along the weir's a tract freer

∞

Has sent
de-centering through the bush
a thorn
tight in the spine
being received by ascension

Carrying
  his own his iron bed
pre-incidences beneath the bin
toad's pin bones

Go tell them
ascending like that protosymbolically

∞

Co-apocalypsing pigeon, eleison with the water's mushrooming into red wash

The twinge with her forearm self-mutilating into all katydid

Has to be veery's
osteoclasts self-suspending
into the susans: crucifixion
then the feathers

—

So
the protocrucifix nestles slick to veery's skeleton
receiving, pitching into the juniper

∞

Serving the arching into hollow eye

Periodizing such red
toward receiving woodpecker
among the grasses
with sun, parousia
struck one step
mitochondria-still
over the bread, removing the bread

Irreduces goldfinch through the yellow parts' salving over
the dormer

∞

Milky the larvae at branch end thinning over position

Effluxus
nonregenerating the bone ends
continually a private
need with the staving off
7mm   When 2 or 3 annul
over blue egg to shape
When 2 or 3 annul over bone graft

Soul all holy city toward terminating in his ribs his red bowl

∞

In out-casting fist perpendicular to the car white seeds
synthesize
furrow over to his arm

The shape
I know door of the sheep
in enough living
flowing from out his belly

The sum dianthus
The sum reappropriating touch
to cover his one hand

Squeeze-flicking upper lip solider is moment

Along my name
    1]   esau
    2] Yellow expending from finch all over hip

∞

Sluicing cockrobin with erythrocytes to englobe how much
more

∞

Last night a pearl-to-lavender grid small in left arm's crook
delimiting into superabundance

Up and along
the trumpet vine
he said roughly
what is invisible fluted
through effluxus with touch
the perimeter the hand
as head of the body
in one portion
stamped on two apple trees
knowing early morning

The trees self-reserve light
with modulating au over to a
in causation

Widens the wood dove
to making distance his tooth

Supersubstantiating "for nine days
the wind hung I to myself"

Speculum

Toc
bunker larkspur
cart cart
value

∞

Bird its use-value coupled to anti-contex
epicenters white in tingle then quartz

A downy gait
however minute

Under thighsun
Only ever arbiter

∞

    Influxus
skimmed with geese
gold flecks
"you will not see my face
but only my back"

Homoousia brighting ladder whole against the house

—Attention
1] compromises the subject/ the object
2] so its anarchy is immediate innate trust
      table the deep spirit moth wing
      as tangerine
      or sun through tulle
      netting along the skin

      Six minutes along skin
3] so attention is anarchy
clasp

    Stitch circular
under wing, blue
lifting, quashing grass
blades with forced-through-the-space

re-radicalizes in approach

∞

Tree's the word cooling to creek water at bottle's metacenter

Category

Stone rolled in front of well
Anamnesis his kiss he wept
from between the tendons

Gathers perception to one flock
An interior object

A means, so has, the sun
from some point on the tree
from chrysarobin

Spelt edom with red mantle

—Little egg's Boolean index the tree

The red the procedural branch
Act supersedes her hair as her mantle

From out Actaeon wood wasp the better in wings in legs in the
wood

In socius the neighbor
metamorphosed to leaf
pupa
The love in socius and neighbor
between
aporia body
politic body

On the one acorn anarration is person

Between two trees
Daphne
Between two likelihoods

∞

    Ideal in the process transvaluing
between the girls
the tree

Sometimes word, sometimes mind, sometimes Jesus,
sometimes door

Necessaries

In gravel
the one point, its femur
supersedes quartz
in the gravel

∞

Kinesthesia
traced fur, glass Polaris
in cognition
to I'm worked   Mouse

—so I'm worked associates
only associates the thumb sized craters
red
with fur, with the rocks around

The love is mosque,
squirrel in the one indentation
above thumb
to be simultaneous
to be bitten into the portion
metatarsal, exuberance

Sometimes the antigens enflame palace on her chest
so a place
Proto-sapient
down filling with influxus
with
a cash under her nail
the marrowy fluid

Sometimes anacoluthon

Haqq
tugs right between owl, the ladder
tugs the skin into cones
ä into etatism

Physiocosmology

θ on the beetle's back
revolatilizes inkling
house peeled to thumb
lli in plurality
outside from rhetoric
a freedom

—In twists-to-them dauber wasps, geist eaten off their wings
—The "with him" down between Y's branches
—If there were mourning doves like this ataraxy

Lord caute
Lord the-flap-over-her-transfigured-muscles
seeing
the small boy's side face to-froing interleukins, aulis

Outside from the word mastery being bluish wing

His ideas, the bee
flat filling between
out from between
bee curving a liquid for his healing

The image as such is usurpation
is retrograde up piercing pine resin
to a density

—Crystalline tract to seize jay
—Messenger's track to seize praxis
self-purifies down along arm a grey-red skin

∞

The speed table, Orion's belt doubling back thumb

Boiling out bridge three boys' front face l circe

In pressing into λ cardinal halves the tree

Curvature

—Inflecting into the line wild hyacinths curl to a crease

—From all veer toward pricked red, toward corncrake is
                                                                the distance
to person

—Radicalizing his hand
1] aims at self-idolatry   Apple
tiling the line over distance to his hand
2] circumscripts oval from the apple

If "God" depends on the divine

"Factual" which in limiting the sheet is his which, his forehead

∞

Being the word mastery, red buttresses into cardinal its wings

∞

Two bees' circle englobes movement-clover, proslogium-clover

∞

  Lord thus
Lord rectilinear box
admit even his hands on the wheelwell

∞

—Curling into the one grub all context

Caress

—'Aql
—A excending her lip as the volume three strands treads back
ownership-iris to possession-iris
—The lowest yellow surface

The image as such self-assembling into pill bug
his touch
Organelle, Sumer for place
Dyad for the angelos

—Lacing out from knee the marrow shapes in Y's tensility
—Dogstar

  Table ordinary out from the spider
being mastery
being integument

—Forms, the same twig arch interpenetrating to person, a
deep blue
onto her chest

On
instead of to go to the house
has posturing oriole Scale
so means the surface

NPaetrisoon

—Archetopos
—Radius all subtle at limestone hyper-centralizing for sky
the belly folded just into the breast
—2 limestones, very fast

∞

—The moon frail area out from garment
—are

∞

Love stet east out from at nest equiliberating sky

At hauls to the one grub 3 or 4 ants

Daisy, day is use temenos
expiating to her breast
seeing yellow glyph
nipple where soul is the risk
use-between

To come to pass
chrysanthemum
two finch eggs
The saying chrysanthemum, the other
denuding skein of sun
red
The word proprioception
would in his hand   the shell
—cadence

—HOURS

that
radiancy&gladness&synklin
are low his bone mass
would
Cup proxy the angelos in

Heliopolis sleeved along arm to ringworm

∞

Near him, form morph from clear hand blue rock touching the sternum

—CHRYSANTHEMUM

—THE LAMP

this presence across the skin of risk
moving temporal image melds right
hand to point

Ψ the liquid environ leaf, ruthmos itself in wind
her wet mouth

∞

RNA, sunboat, the bunkering in on arm

Secrus judicat orbis terrarum

—Window box binding over moist nest, Charybdis
—Copper thread flush under one
the reddening up to touch
her back in proportion to her legs

∞

Alighted from ringworm hand, eye initially
the raising circle
—warm
—rain

Shake dove from endurance, beacon after form into hauled
into the bird

His conflation an impromtu liquid
tongue both inner the organ outward
Diorite

∞

Her lip at buoyance limits through horizon
each
corpse lion
the house the robbers the field

Of course saying mouth concresces into red cedar bowls
ample wrong names
making stand sun
 in each crevice

∞

Becoming standing still was the wood
Connection, surfaces bit from between her fingers

Oxyrhynchus

Sore making half squash blossom, the accident in it, Eros

1] Extricating on from robin
2] rib branch of
3] Polyphemus

Succession at his finger
the he's bleeding arriving
forest
Plain skin being motion

Vox bête cove
The small of her back coming east toward, up from the bed

Foot chortle   The pulling toward

Uvula truncating into her collar even

Her arm the unit, voyeurism

Sign of accordance

Producing lifting logorhythm   the jasmine sucked up from
the ground

Enchainment

Yellow bird sunk then up autonotion to being grip

Bringing materiality, the taking wasp from his hand
Quartz bringing mirrorical drops
being chair

Re-tenses into thumb at triangles to the bamboo
the saying conflagrant into her collar well

∞

His pushing in her being recorder, white car

Seeing crow limbs the word for it, bulbing up to folk from
the table

∞

Public vision

∞

Anticipating knee, the moving her leg into breast

FOCUSING THE MOVING IN TWITCH
FOOT OPENING FROM HIM   THE BENCH

Duplicate

Contracting into palm the fingers over her hair
Blue loop, grammar in which horse

FOCUSING THE MOVING CURLS HER HAND INTO ITSELF
UP AND OUT FROM THE MIRROR
IN ON TOUCH ALL OVER HIP

HUNG ARM PIT RECORDER ADEQUATING KNEE IN HER
—The two solid bands of rain water

DURING FOCUSING THE MOVING ON THROUGH THE HOUSE
WINDOW HAND INFOLDING TO DOVES CREVICE

THE ARCHING UP BACK FROM THEN INTO BUTTOCK ARMS
SYLLOGISM TOPOI THE CANTERING FORWARD LEVEL SKIN

—Watcher
—Fig, where it is abutment

SUN BACKLIGHTING THE CELL HIS PANOPTIC VISION

GLASSBODY HAVING THE TURNING INTO OVERSEER
GLASSBODY HAVING THE TURNING INTO COMRADE

BE HIS HAND MOVING AGAINST SHELL

TOWELING REFRACTING INTO SKINFOOTRUG ACTAEON
VOICE ACTION

About the Author

Lance Phillips was born in Germany in 1970. A graduate of the University of North Carolina and the Iowa Writers' Workshop, he lives in Greensboro, North Carolina, with his wife and son.

Ahsahta Press

New Series

Lance Phillips, *Corpus Socius*

Modern and Contemporary Poetry of the American West

Sandra Alcosser, *A Fish to Feed All Hunger*
David Axelrod, *Jerusalem of Grass*
David Baker, *Laws of the Land*
Dick Barnes, *Few and Far Between*
Conger Beasley, Jr., *Over DeSoto's Bones*
Linda Bierds, *Flights of the Harvest-Mare*
Richard Blessing, *Winter Constellations*
Boyer, Burmaster, and Trusky, eds., *The Ahsahta Anthology*
Peggy Pond Church, *New and Selected Poems*
Katharine Coles, *The One Right Touch*
Wyn Cooper, *The Country of Here Below*
Craig Cotter, *Chopstix Numbers*
Judson Crews, *The Clock of Moss*
H.L. Davis, *Selected Poems*
Susan Strayer Deal, *The Dark is a Door*
Susan Strayer Deal, *No Moving Parts*
Linda Dyer, *Fictional Teeth*
Gretel Ehrlich, *To Touch the Water*
Gary Esarey, *How Crows Talk and Willows Walk*
Julie Fay, *Portraits of Women*
Thomas Hornsby Ferril, *Anvil of Roses*
Thomas Hornsby Ferril, *Westering*

HILDEGARDE FLANNER, *The Hearkening Eye*
CHARLEY JOHN GREASYBEAR, *Songs*
CORRINNE HALES, *Underground*
HAZEL HALL, *Selected Poems*
NAN HANNON, *Sky River*
GWENDOLEN HASTE, *Selected Poems*
KEVIN HEARLE, *Each Thing We Know Is Changed Because We Know It And Other Poems*
SONYA HESS, *Kingdom of Lost Waters*
CYNTHIA HOGUE, *The Woman in Red*
ROBERT KRIEGER, *Headlands, Rising*
ELIO EMILIANO LIGI, *Disturbances*
HANIEL LONG, *My Seasons*
KEN MCCULLOUGH, *Sycamore•Oriole*
NORMAN MCLEOD, *Selected Poems*
BARBARA MEYN, *The Abalone Heart*
DAVID MUTSCHLECNER, *Esse*
DIXIE PARTRIDGE, *Deer in the Haystacks*
GERRYE PAYNE, *The Year-God*
GEORGE PERREAULT, *Curved Like an Eye*
HOWARD W. ROBERTSON, *to the fierce guard in the Assyrian Saloon*
LEO ROMERO, *Agua Negra*
LEO ROMERO, *Going Home Away Indian*
MIRIAM SAGAN, *The Widow's Coat*
PHILIP ST. CLAIR, *At the Tent of Heaven*
PHILIP ST. CLAIR, *Little-Dog-of-Iron*
DONALD SCHENKER, *Up Here*
GARY SHORT, *Theory of Twilight*
D.J. SMITH, *Prayers for the Dead Ventriloquist*
RICHARD SPEAKES, *Hannah's Travel*

Genevieve Taggard, *To the Natural World*
Tom Trusky, ed., *Women Poets of the West*
Marnie Walsh, *A Taste of the Knife*
Bill Witherup, *Men at Work*
Carolyne Wright, *Stealing the Children*

This book is set in Apollo type with New Baskerville titles
by Ahsahta Press at Boise State University
and manufactured on acid-free paper
by the Boise State University Print Shop,
Boise, Idaho.

AHSAHTA PRESS
2002

JANET HOLMES, DIRECTOR

CAROLYN FRITSCHLE
JOSH KENNEDY
FARGO KESEY
RUSSELL KING
SHANNON MAHONEY
WILLIAM GUY MILLER
MAURA PAYNE
MATT REITER

ANTHONY HADLEY, INTERN